# COUNTRY FACT FILES

# Germany

## David Flint

## MACDONALD YOUNG BOOKS

First published in 1992 by Simon & Schuster Young Books

Reprinted in 1994 by Macdonald Young Books

First published in paperback in 1998 by Macdonald Young Books

Macdonald Young Books,
an imprint of Wayland Publishers
61 Western Road
Hove
East Sussex
BN3 1JD

Find Macdonald Young Books on the internet at:
http://www.myb.co.uk

| | |
|---|---|
| **Design** | Roger Kohn |
| **Consultant** | David Burtenshaw, Principal Lecturer in Geography |
| **Editor** | Penny Clarke |
| **DTP editor** | Helen Swansbourne |
| **Picture research** | Valerie Mulcahy |
| **Illustration** | Janos Marffy |

We are grateful to the following for permission
to reproduce photographs:

Front cover: Kaiser Wilhelm I Church, Berlin, Telegraph Colour Library and Gisela Floto for children photograph; Camera Press, page 8 (Jonathan Haddock); J Allan Cash, page 17; Robert Harding Picture Library, pages 15, 21, 29, 31, 36; The Image Bank, pages 35 (Gary Cralle), 38 (Hans Wolf); Magnum Photos, page 39 (James Nachtwey); Marco Polo, page 42 (F Bouilot); Picturepoint, page 18 (Dr Reinbacher); Rex Features, pages 19 (Cham), 25 *above* (Boccon Glbod), 25 *below* (Francois Lehr); Caroline Salguero/Odyssey/TRIP, page 20; Select, page 23 (Dirk Robbers); Spectrum Colour Library, pages 8/9 (JRaga), 34; Tony Stone Worldwide, pages 10, 11 (Manfred Mehlig), 22, 33, 40, 41 (Charles Thatcher); Zefa, pages 12 (Rossenbach), 13 (Sharp Shooters), 14 (J Pfaff), 16 (F Damm), 27 (F Damm), 28, 30 (Streichen), 32 (Justitz), 37 (Streichan), 43.

Printed in Hong Kong by Wing King Tong Ltd

A CIP catalogue record for this book is available from the British Library

ISBN: 0 7500 2612 X

**C O N T E N T S**

Words that are explained in the glossary are printed in
SMALL CAPITALS the first time they are mentioned in the text.

# ▬ INTRODUCTION

Germany is a large, powerful and important country. It has close links with its neighbours and is a leading member of the group of countries which make up the European Community (EC). Germany is at the heart of Europe, stretching 800 kilometres from the Baltic coast in the north to the Austrian border in the south. From the Polish border in the east it stretches 700 kilometres west to the Netherlands.

Germany has not always been a large, united country. For much of its early history it was made up of many small separate independent states, each with its own ruling family. In 1871 Bismarck, the German Chancellor, finally managed to unite all these states into one Germany. Between 1914 and 1945 Germany fought and lost two world wars. Germany supported Austria against Russia in 1914 and this led to the First World War. France, Great Britain, Russia and the USA finally won this conflict in 1918.

In 1933 Adolf Hitler and the Nazi party came to power in Germany. Hitler built up a powerful army, navy and air force with which to conquer Europe. In 1939 Germany invaded Poland, so starting the Second World War. Germany was finally defeated

◀ *The Berlin Wall symbolized Germany's division into two countries: East Germany and West Germany. It was finally demolished in 1990.*

by Great Britain, the Soviet Union and the USA in 1945.

As a result of that defeat Germany became divided into two countries: East Germany and West Germany. These developed separately, with their own governments. East Germany had a communist government while West Germany was a western-style democracy. By 1989 people in East Germany had decided they wanted a different form of government. There were marches and protests which forced the government to make changes. Finally, in 1990, the two Germanys were reunited.

◀ *The Brandenburg Gate was the busiest crossroads in Europe before 1939. Then it became the dividing line between East and West. Now, once again, it bustles with life.*

# THE LANDSCAPE

Germany is a country of broad plains, thick forests, deep valleys and high mountains. The highest mountain peaks are in the Alps or the Erzebirge (Ore Mountains) of southern Germany. The thick forests of the mountains' lower slopes give way to meadows. Many flowers, such as the famous blue gentian, used to be found in these meadows, but their numbers have been reduced by farmers using artificial fertilisers and PESTICIDES. Higher still the meadows give way to bare rocky slopes, covered with ice at the very highest levels.

Central Germany has high plains, valleys and forests. The rivers Rhine and Elbe carve their way across the region, providing routes for main roads and railways.

In the past most of Germany was covered by forests of birch, beech and oak. A lot of this woodland has been cut down for farms, towns and factories, but there are still important woodland areas like the Black Forest.

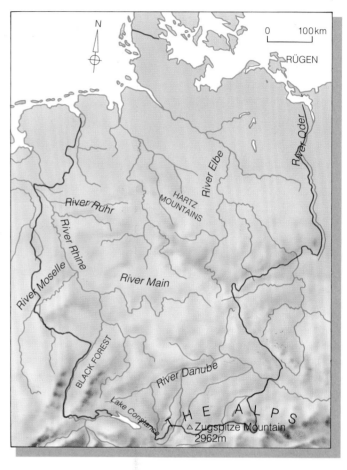

◄*High mountains, with glaciers and waterfalls, make the German Alps a popular tourist area all the year round.*

▲*The river systems that flow from Germany's mountains and across the country's wide plains have always been an important means of transport and communications across Europe.*

In the last hundred years many of the areas of natural forest have been replanted with faster growing coniferous trees like pine, fir and spruce. Over half the country's forests have been planted in this way, especially in the south and east.

▲ *The river Rhine is one of Germany's most important waterways. It links northern and southern Europe and is used by thousands of barges transporting goods.*

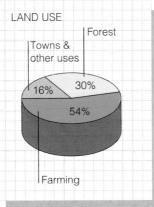

LAND USE

Towns & other uses
Forest
16%
30%
54%
Farming

North Germany is an area of low hills, flat plains, shallow lakes and marshes. On the Baltic coast there are long stretches of fine sand popular with summer holidaymakers. Rügen is a low chalk island in the Baltic Sea separated from the mainland by a narrow channel.

# KEY FACTS ON RIVERS

● The river Rhine flows north and west and is 1,320 kilometres long.
● The river Elbe, an important river flowing from south-east to north-west, is 1,167 kilometres long.
● The river Danube rises in the south-west of Germany and flows for 1,287 kilometres east through seven other countries to the Black Sea.

# KEY FACTS ON LAKES

● Lake Constance: 538.5 square kilometres
● Lake Muritz: 115.3 square kilometres
● Lake Chiemsee: 82.0 square kilometres
● Lake Schwerinersee 65.5 square kilometres

# CLIMATE AND WEATHER

Climatically Germany is at the point in Europe where the warm, wet conditions coming from the west meet the colder, drier conditions coming from the east. Because of this, the climate and weather varies from year to year. In some years winters are bitterly cold and dry, while in other years milder, wetter winters can be expected.

In general, southern Germany is warmer for most of the year than the north. However this general pattern is influenced by altitude. Over much of the country people live and work in areas which are well over 450 metres above sea level. Temperatures fall by 1°C for every 150 metres of altitude. This means that places on the Rhine plateau, for example, are 3°C to 4°C colder than nearby Cologne. Higher areas also tend to have heavier rain and snow falls throughout the year. This is

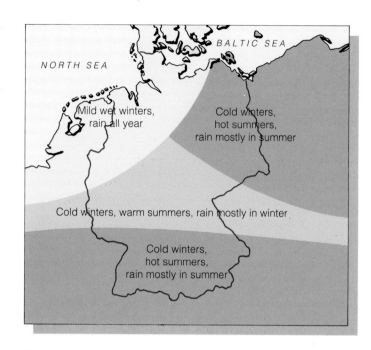

▲ *East and south Germany have colder winters but warmer summers than the north and west.*

▼ *Hamburg's rain falls all year round, but Berlin gets most of its rain in the summer months.*

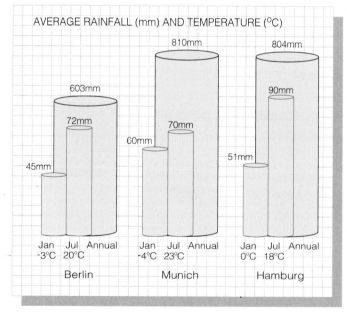

AVERAGE RAINFALL (mm) AND TEMPERATURE (°C)

Berlin: 45mm (Jan -3°C), 72mm (Jul 20°C), 603mm Annual
Munich: 60mm (Jan -4°C), 70mm (Jul 23°C), 810mm Annual
Hamburg: 51mm (Jan 0°C), 90mm (Jul 18°C), 804mm Annual

◀ *Hot, sunny summers allow both red and white grapes to ripen even in central parts of the country. German wine is famous all over the world.*

because rainfall increases when rain-bearing winds are forced to rise over highland areas like the Black Forest.

Northern and western parts of Germany are affected by the moderating influence of the sea. The sea tends to make winters milder and summers cooler than places further inland. As a result the central and eastern regions, unaffected by the influence of the sea, have cold winters but hot summers. These central and eastern areas also have a shorter growing season and more days with frost each year: Cologne has 44 frost days, but in contrast Berlin has 90.

▼ *Cold, snowy winters mean that many Germans are keen skiers. Cross-country skiing (called* LANGLAUF*) is popular with people of all ages.*

## KEY FACTS

● Western parts of Germany are about 100mm a year wetter than the eastern parts.
● Rainfall varies according to position. Places like Koblenz in the Rhine valley have 1000mm less rainfall a year than the surrounding hills.
● In the Rhine valley apple trees start to flower around 20 April but in colder Berlin they do not start until after 9 May.

# NATURAL RESOURCES

The economic growth of Germany since 1945 has been based on energy from coal, oil, gas and nuclear power. Germany has both black coal and brown coal (lignite). The largest black coalfield is the Ruhr in the west of the country. The Ruhr provided the power for German industries and towns throughout the 19th century and it is still important. The early coal mines were in the southern part of the field where the coal was found on the surface. Now mining is concentrated in deep mines in the north of the coalfield.

Brown coal, or lignite, is extracted from huge OPEN-CAST MINES. One near Cologne will cover an area the size of Birmingham. Most lignite is burnt in power stations.

Germany has no oil, so this fuel has to be imported. Some comes by pipeline from the CIS (Commonwealth of Independent States) and the North Sea. The rest is imported from the Middle East and South America (the OPEC countries), and comes by barge and pipeline via the port of Rotterdam in the Netherlands. About 60 per cent of Germany's natural gas is imported from the Netherlands and the North Sea, the rest comes from the Middle East and Siberia in the CIS.

Many nuclear power stations were built during the last 20 years. The aim was to reduce Germany's dependence on imported fuels like oil and natural gas. However nuclear power stations are very expensive to build and the public is concerned about the dangers of an accidental release of radioactivity. Disposing of the radioactive waste from these power stations is also a problem. As a result, Germany has stopped building nuclear power stations.

Hydro-electricity is an important source of power in parts of south Germany, where

▼ *Open-cast brown coal mining is much cheaper than deep coal mining but can do great damage to the environment.*

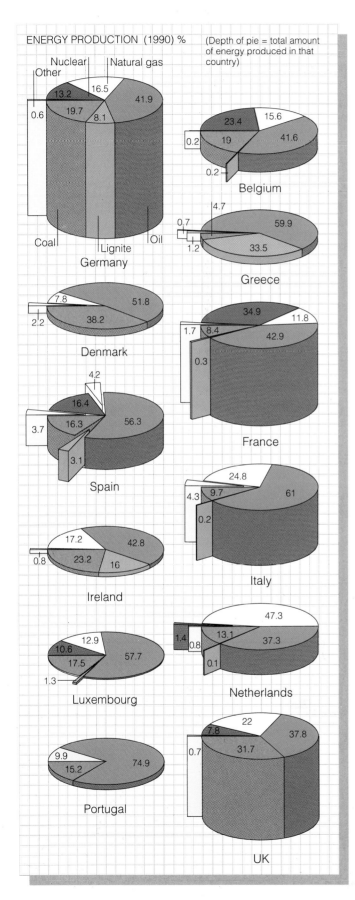

ENERGY PRODUCTION (1990) %

(Depth of pie = total amount of energy produced in that country)

**Germany**
Nuclear
Other
Natural gas
13.2  16.5
0.6  19.7  8.1  41.9
Coal  Lignite  Oil

**Belgium**
23.4  15.6
0.2  19  41.6
0.2

**Greece**
4.7
0.7  59.9
1.2  33.5

**Denmark**
7.8  51.8
2.2  38.2

**France**
34.9  11.8
1.7  8.4  42.9
0.3

**Spain**
4.2
16.4  56.3
3.7  16.3
3.1

**Italy**
24.8
4.3  9.7  61
0.2

**Ireland**
17.2  42.8
0.8  23.2  16

**Netherlands**
47.3
1.4  13.1  37.3
0.8
0.1

**Luxembourg**
12.9
10.6  57.7
17.5
1.3

**Portugal**
9.9  74.9
15.2

**UK**
22
7.8  37.8
0.7  31.7

there are fast flowing rivers. Hydro-electric power stations are expensive to build but cheap to run because the fuel (water) is free. Germany is also experimenting with generating power from the wind and the sun.

Germany's forests are another important resource. Over a million trees are cut down every year for furniture, paper-making or house-building. The government encourages forest owners to plant more trees than they fell.

▼ **Germany is experimenting with wind power. This is an important form of** RENEWABLE ENERGY.

# POPULATION

*◄ About 60 per cent of Germans live in main cities. During the Second World War many towns and cities were badly damaged but these have been carefully rebuilt.*

*▼ Hamburg, Berlin and Munich are Germany's largest cities with populations of over one million.*

After Germany was unified in 1871 the country's population grew by over a million each year until 1912. By 1939 Germany had a population of 43 million. After the Second World War the country was divided into two states, and the city of Berlin was also divided. The area of Germany controlled by the Russian forces became East Germany, with East Berlin as its capital. The area controlled by the Allies (Great Britain, the USA and France)

## KEY FACTS

- Population (in millions)
1989 West Germany 64.17
     East Germany 16.4
1990 United Germany 78.5
1991 United Germany 79.15
1990 Annual average income per person
    US$ 12,080 (in the USA the figure
    is $23,150)
1990 People per square kilometre 221
- 1990 Religions (%)
Christianity 91 (Protestant 65, Catholic 26)
Other 9

0    100km

□ Hamburg
● Bremen
▲ Hanover
■ Berlin
▲ Magdeburg
● Dortmund
● Düsseldorf
● Cologne
Halle ●
● Leipzig
Jena ●
Dresden ●
● Frankfurt
▲ Mannheim
▲ Nuremberg
● Stuttgart
Munich □

■ Over 2 million
□ 1–2 million
● 500,000–1million
▲ 200,000–500,000

▶ *The countryside is a very important part of German life, both for producing food and as a place for recreation.*

became West Germany, with Bonn as its capital. West Berlin, although surrounded by East Germany, was a part of West Germany.

The movement of people and goods between the two parts of the country became very difficult. Large numbers of East Germans disliked the new communist state and fled to West Germany. Many of these refugees were doctors, teachers, health workers, scientists and other people vital to East Germany. So, on 13 August 1961, the

East Germans built the Berlin Wall to stop people escaping to the West. The whole frontier between the two countries was lined, on the East German side, by barbed wire and watchtowers and guarded by armed soldiers with fierce dogs.

Despite these measures East Germany's population declined as people still found ways to escape. Between 1961 and 1989 74 people were killed trying to escape from East to West Berlin. In contrast West Germany's population grew as the country's economy boomed.

Since reunification in 1990 Germany's population has continued to grow but the rate of increase is slowing. People are also living longer thanks to advances in medicine. This means there will be an increasing number of old people who will need to be cared for in the future.

◀ *Communist East Germany's population declined by 1.6 million between 1950 and 1989, but West Germany's grew by over 10 million.*

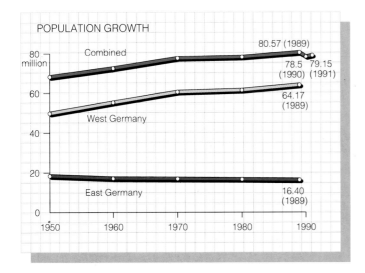

POPULATION GROWTH

Combined — 80.57 (1989)
78.5 (1990) 79.15 (1991)

West Germany — 64.17 (1989)

East Germany — 16.40 (1989)

80 million · 60 · 40 · 20 · 0

1950 · 1960 · 1970 · 1980 · 1990

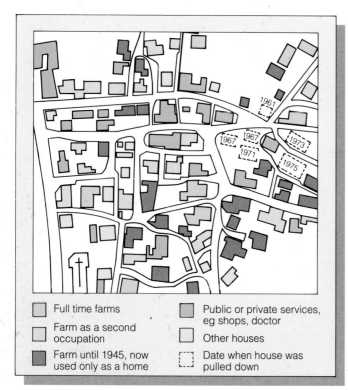

▲ **With more elderly people treatments using spa water are becoming increasingly popular.**

▼ **German villages have fewer farms than 20 years ago. For more and more people farming is only a secondary occupation.**

| | | | |
|---|---|---|---|
| ☐ | Full time farms | ☐ | Public or private services, eg shops, doctor |
| ☐ | Farm as a second occupation | ☐ | Other houses |
| ☐ | Farm until 1945, now used only as a home | ⌐⌐ | Date when house was pulled down |

Some people in Germany are leaving towns to live in villages in the nearby countryside. They feel that rural areas offer more peace and quiet with less pollution and a better quality of life. So farms in villages close to towns are bought by city dwellers who sell the land and often redesign the buildings. During the day these villages are very quiet when everyone has gone to work and life only revives in the evening when people return.

People in Germany are also concerned about the issue of FOREIGN WORKERS in their country. Throughout the 1960s and 1970s German economic growth was rapid. One result of this was that people from the poorer countries of Europe, like Turkey and Portugal, moved to Germany in search of better paid jobs. Many Germans did not want to do the dirtier, unskilled, often dangerous jobs like refuse disposal. At this stage the foreign workers were made welcome. Usually, just one person from a family moved to Germany, then after a few years other family members joined them.

The problem has not been helped by German re-unification. The problems of integrating the bustling, prosperous western part of the country with the much poorer, run-down eastern part are enormous.

Today, the country's economic growth is slower and many Germans have lost their jobs. These unemployed people often resent foreign workers who, they feel, are stealing their jobs. Foreign workers usually live in big cities, where they keep their own language, culture and religion. Their lifestyle is different from that of local people. In some places this has created social tensions. High concentrations of foreign workers can make local people feel outnumbered. For example 70 per cent of all pupils in Frankfurt's primary schools come from the families of foreign workers.

Life is not easy for foreign workers. Many cannot afford the fare to visit relatives so feelings of homesickness are common. Demonstrations against these workers can lead to violence and there are programmes to persuade some of them to return home.

▶ *Most of Germany's foreign workers come from the poorer countries of southern Europe.*

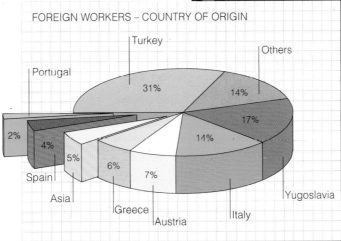

FOREIGN WORKERS – COUNTRY OF ORIGIN

Turkey 31%
Others 14%
17%
14%
Portugal
2%
4%
5%
6%
7%
Spain
Asia
Greece
Austria
Italy
Yugoslavia

▶ *Foreign workers came mainly to do the jobs that Germans were un-willing to do. Now that unemployment among German people has increased, foreign workers have become unpopular because German workers feel that jobs should be re-served for Germans.*

# DAILY LIFE

Children usually attend kindergartens or nursery schools when they are three years old. Germany was the first country to introduce schooling for young children, but the system has now spread to many other countries. Some nursery schools are free, but in others parents have to pay. Children start primary school when they are six. When they are ten they go to a GYMNASIUM (grammar school), a REALSCHULE (middle school), or HAUPTSCHULE (secondary school). Each type of school provides general education and training, though the Hauptschule and Realschule tend to concentrate on technical skills. At 18 students who want to go to university take an exam called the ABITUR.

The school day starts at 7.30 am in summer and 8 am in winter and ends in the early afternoon. Then children go home for lunch. There is a mid-morning break of about 30 minutes when children eat the sandwiches they have brought. This is called the 'second breakfast'. Usually there are lessons on Saturday mornings.

Workers in Germany's factories and offices now have at least four weeks paid holiday each year. Until the 1970s people worked a 40-hour week, but now a 36-hour week is quite common. As a result people have more free time for their leisure interests.

Germans enjoy both watching and talking part in many sports, from football to sailing, skiing and cycling. In towns there are keep fit trails (*Trimmdich-pfade*) in parks and wooded areas. Football is the most popular spectator sport, followed by gymnastics. Special classes in sport help pupils to develop their skills from an early age.

▶ *The different types of school in Germany.*

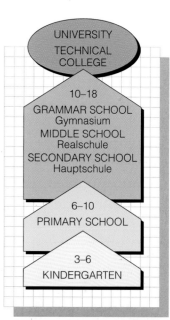

UNIVERSITY
TECHNICAL
COLLEGE

10–18
GRAMMAR SCHOOL
Gymnasium
MIDDLE SCHOOL
Realschule
SECONDARY SCHOOL
Hauptschule

6–10
PRIMARY SCHOOL

3–6
KINDERGARTEN

▼ *Science and technology take up 15% of the school timetable. Science fairs like this one are popular with all ages.*

## KEY FACTS

● Between 1970 and 1990 the number of schoolchildren in West Germany fell by 2 million to 8.8 million. In East Germany the fall was 800,000 to 2.5 million.
● The most frequent cause of death in Germany in 1991 was heart attacks, followed by cancer.

▼ *Football is the most popular spectator sport in Germany and over 200,000 people see a match each weekend. There were great celebrations throughout the country when Germany won the World Cup in 1990.*

RECREATION AREAS IN THE RUHR

River Rhine

River Lippe

River Emscher

● Dortmund

River Ruhr

Essen ● ● Bochum

Duisburg ●

■ Towns and cities
■ Green areas – parks
— Border of Ruhr planning region

0  10 km

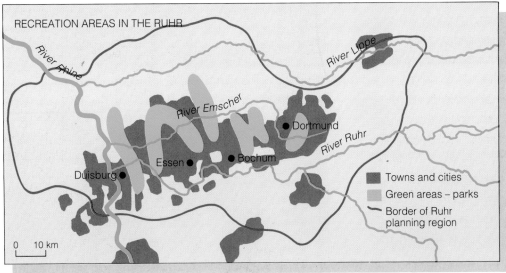

◄ *An important industrial area, the Ruhr is one of the most densely populated parts of Germany. To improve the region green areas have been created to separate the towns and cities and over 27 million trees have been planted.*

There are many festivals and celebrations throughout the year in Germany. Many of these festivals date back to pre-Christian or medieval times. Particular parts of the country are famous for their festivals, for example the *Oktoberfest* in Munich. During September many villages and towns in the wine-making areas celebrate a good harvest with their WEINFEST.

A new holiday or festival, celebrating the reunification of the country, is held on 3 October. Easter is an important festival and on Easter Sunday children search their gardens for Easter eggs 'planted' by their parents.

Germans are great readers, perhaps because printing was invented here in the

▲ *The Beer Hall is crammed during the famous Munich Beer Festival held in October each year. Thousands of people from many parts of the world travel to Munich to take part in the Oktoberfest.*

15th century. At least 10 per cent of all books published in the world are written in German, which is also an important language for papers on scientific research.

Germany's two national television companies provide three channels. Channels One and Two are for national programmes, while Channel Three covers local issues. Cable and satellite television are becoming increasingly common.

| DAILY LIFE STATISTICS | 1970 and 1980 figures for W Germany | | |
| | 1990 figures for united Germany | | |
| --- | --- | --- | --- |
| | 1970 | 1980 | 1990* |
| **Theatres** | | | |
| No. of public theatres | 194 | 221 | 410 |
| No. of people attending | 17.6m | 17.3m | 21.4m |
| **Cinemas** | | | |
| Number of cinemas | 3,597 | 3,354 | 4,127 |
| **Book publishing** | | | |
| First editions published | 38,703 | 54,572 | 60,175 |
| **Newspapers** | | | |
| No. of newspapers | 375 | 368 | 397 |
| No. of magazines | 5,142 | 6,243 | 8,197 |
| **Youth hostels** | | | |
| No. of hostels | 633 | 566 | 604 |
| **Sports associations** | | | |
| No. of sports clubs | 39,201 | 53,451 | 75,652 |
| Club members | 8.3m | 14.4m | 21.3m |

▼ **This newstand in Berlin is typical of many throughout the country. It sells a wide range of newspapers and magazines.**

# KEY FACTS

● Every day the German people buy 30 million newspapers.

● The tabloid newspaper *Bild Zeitung* is read by over 7 million people a day.

● 70% of Germans order their daily newspaper from a local newsagent.

● Some famous newspapers are based in one city like the *Hamburger Abendblatt* and *Frankfurter Allgemeine Zeitung*.

● The festival of *Karneval*, or *Fasching* as it is called in southern Germany, takes place on the three days before Ash Wednesday. There are street parties, fancy dress competitions and parades.

# RULE AND LAW

Germany has a federal system of government very similar to the USA. The country is divided into 16 LÄNDER or states which have a great deal of power in their areas. People in the different Länder have strong feelings of independence and local identity. For example, people in the south often refer to themselves as Bavarians first and Germans second.

In Germany, like the UK, people can vote from the age of 18. At elections everyone has two votes. One is for a local candidate to represent them in the regional Länder government. The other is for a candidate from a national political party to represent them in the BUNDESTAG, the German equivalent of the British House of Commons and the US Congress.

Members of each Länder government appoint members to represent them and their state in the BUNDESRAT. This is the upper house of the German Parliament, and so like the House of Lords in the UK and the House of Representatives in the USA. It looks very closely at laws passed by the Bundestag.

*Germany is divided into 16 Länder or regional states. These vary greatly in size, number of cities, population and degree of industrialisation.*

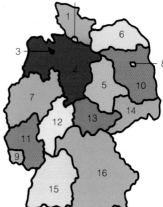

## KEY FACTS

● Germans regard voting as an important duty and over 80% register their choice in national and local elections.
● Political power is divided between the central government and the Länder.
● The head of state is the Federal President. He or she represents the country in national matters.
● The Federal President is elected for five years by the Federal Convention.

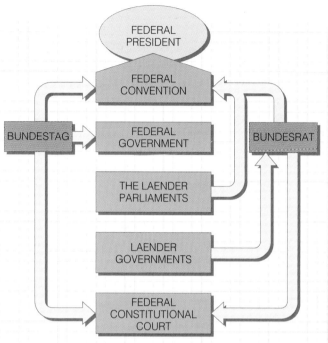

Head of state is the federal president, elected for 5 years by the federal convention.

The federal convention is made up of all members of the Bundestag and an equal number of members elected by the Laender parliaments.

▲*The number of seats in the Bundestag had to be increased from 519 to 663 in 1990 when the country was reunified. The Bundestag moved from Bonn to its new home in Berlin.*

▼*The German armed forces are part of NATO (North Atlantic Treaty Organization) which includes the U.S., U.K., and other European countries.*

The chief political parties are the Christian Democratic Union (CDU), the Social Democratic Party (SPD), and the Free Democratic Party (FDP). To have any seats in the Bundestag a political party must win five percent of the votes throughout the country. This is hard on small parties like the ecological Green Party.

The head of state is the federal president but he or she has little political power. The real power is held by the chancellor, who is elected by the members of the Bundestag at the suggestion of the federal president. In practice, the chancellor is the head of the party that has won most votes in the election. The chancellor appoints the ministers of government.

The Federal Constitutional Court is the highest court in Germany. It deals with disputes between the central government and the Laender.

# ◼ FOOD AND FARMING

In the west and south of Germany farms are small, covering between 25 and 50 hectares. Despite this, the farms are highly efficient, with the result that Germany produces 75 per cent of its own food. There are still some of the traditional tiny German farms of less than 10 hectares. Most of these are worked part-time by people who also have another job. Overall, 65 per cent of all farmers have a second job.

In the eastern regions the large state and COLLECTIVE FARMS used to be owned by the government. These are being broken up into smaller units, and sold to co-operative groups of farmers. In the past the government in these eastern areas dictated what crops to grow and which animals to keep. Now individual farmers and FARMING CO-OPERATIVES are free to decide for themselves.

The cool, damp conditions throughout most of Germany encourage the growth of grass for DAIRY FARMING or cereals like wheat and barley for ARABLE FARMING.

In the cool, wet part of northern Germany rye and oats used to be important crops. Today, however, fewer farmers grow them because plant breeders have developed types of wheat and barley that will thrive in the more northern areas and both these crops are more useful than oats and rye.

Sugar beet and cereals are grown on the plains and lowlands of northern Germany as food for cattle reared for their milk and meat.

In southern Germany the hotter summers mean that maize can be grown for feeding to cattle and pigs. Most pigs are reared in intensive units to meet the large demand for pork and Wurst (sausages). Pig rearing has increased by 40 per cent in the last 10 years.

Vines are an important crop on sunny, south-facing slopes in the Rhine and Moselle valleys. Steep hillsides are terraced to create flat land for the vines. Traditionally, Rhine wine is sold in brown bottles and Moselle in green ones.

FARM SIZES (hectares)

1970
over 20 ha    |5–20 ha
16.4
14.3    23.1    46.2

1–2 ha    2–5 ha

1980
26.3
12.9    19.1    41.7

1990
(United Germany)
45.1
10.1    14.2    30.6

◀ *West Germany was a country of small farms while East Germany had large state-owned farms. Now many small farms are being amalgamated.*

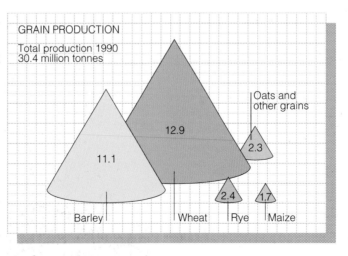

GRAIN PRODUCTION

Total production 1990
30.4 million tonnes

Oats and other grains

12.9

11.1    2.3

2.4    1.7

Barley    Wheat    Rye    Maize

◀ *Wheat is Germany's main grain crop and production is increasing. Much of the wheat goes to make flour. Barley is mostly used for brewing beer or processing into animal feed.*

| PRODUCTION OF CEREALS IN THE EC, USA AND JAPAN, 1990 (million tonnes) | | | | |
|---|---|---|---|---|
| | Wheat | Barley | Oats | Maize |
| Germany | 14.1 | 11.1 | 3.3 | 1.9 |
| Belgium | 1.2 | 0.7 | 0.07 | 0.05 |
| Denmark | 2.1 | 4.9 | 0.1 | – |
| Greece | 2.3 | 0.6 | 0.06 | 2.1 |
| Spain | 5.6 | 9.8 | 0.5 | 3.6 |
| France | 27.8 | 10.2 | 1.4 | 12.8 |
| Ireland | 0.4 | 1.5 | 0.1 | – |
| Italy | 8.9 | 1.6 | 0.3 | 6.2 |
| Luxembourg | 0.03 | 0.06 | 0.2 | – |
| Netherlands | 0.8 | 0.02 | 0.05 | – |
| Portugal | 0.5 | 0.07 | 0.13 | 0.6 |
| UK | 12.5 | 9.3 | 0.5 | 0.04 |
| EC | 76.23 | 49.85 | 6.71 | 27.29 |
| USA | 54.5 | 10.4 | 4.7 | 171.4 |
| Japan | 1.0 | 0.3 | – | – |

▲ *This combine harvester is working in Schleswig-Holstein. Large machines need large fields so fences and hedges between fields have been removed.*

# KEY FACTS

● Only 5% of Germans now work in agriculture. In 1960 the figure was 20%.

● The number of farms decreased from 2.1 million in 1950 to 650,000 in 1990.

● Germany has over 23 million pigs, 20 million cattle and 1.1 million sheep.

▲*In modern milking parlours cows get a measured ration of food during milking.*

▼*Germany and France dominate meat and milk production in the EC.*

German breakfasts usually consist of brown or white rolls with jam, marmalade, butter, coffee and perhaps a boiled egg or cold meat. Because people have to leave home around 7.30 am for school or work most take sandwiches and a drink to have at mid-morning. Lunch is the most important meal of the day. There is usually a meat dish, with cooked vegetables, potatoes and gravy. Pork is the most popular meat, followed by veal, chicken and beef. The evening meal usually consists of a selection of cold meats together with

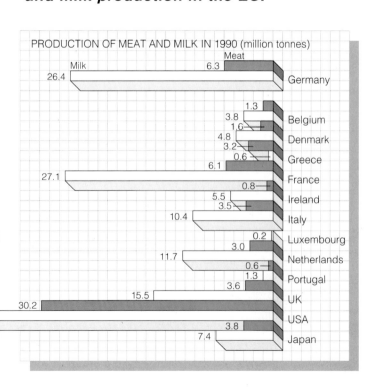

PRODUCTION OF MEAT AND MILK IN 1990 (million tonnes)

Meat

Milk

| | Milk | Meat | |
|---|---|---|---|
| Germany | 26.4 | 6.3 | |
| Belgium | 3.8 | 1.3 | |
| Denmark | 4.8 | 1.6 | |
| Greece | 3.2 | 0.6 | |
| France | 27.1 | 6.1 | |
| Ireland | 5.5 | 0.8 | |
| Italy | 10.4 | 3.5 | |
| Luxembourg | | 0.2 | |
| Netherlands | 11.7 | 3.0 | |
| Portugal | | 0.6 | |
| UK | 15.5 | 3.6 | |
| USA | 64.7 | 30.2 | |
| Japan | 7.4 | 3.8 | |

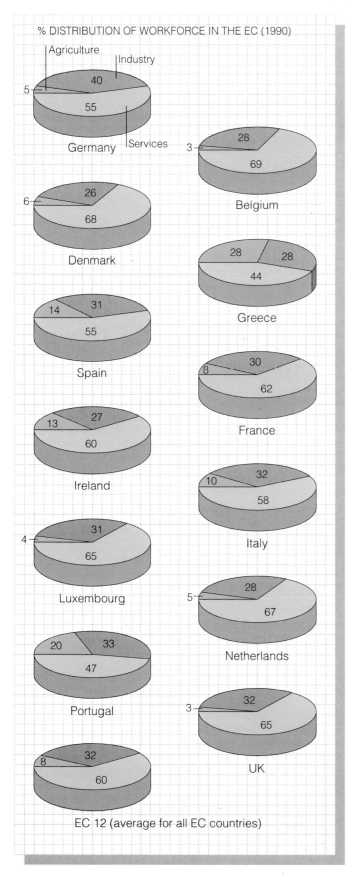

% DISTRIBUTION OF WORKFORCE IN THE EC (1990)

Agriculture
Industry

Germany — 5, 40, 55, Services

Belgium — 3, 28, 69

Denmark — 6, 26, 68

Greece — 28, 28, 44

Spain — 14, 31, 55

France — 8, 30, 62

Ireland — 13, 27, 60

Italy — 10, 32, 58

Luxembourg — 4, 31, 65

Netherlands — 5, 28, 67

Portugal — 20, 33, 47

UK — 3, 32, 65

EC 12 (average for all EC countries) — 8, 32, 60

bread, cheese and fruit.

Sausages are a German speciality, especially the famous Frankfurter. Each part of the country has its favourite sausage recipe and many regions brew their own local beers. These have now become popular in other countries.

The different parts of Germany have become famous for particular types of food. In the north, near the sea, fish dishes with eels and lobster are popular. In Westphalia, in the north-west, fine smoked ham is served with pumpernickel, a brown rye bread. Munich is famous for its white sausages. The *enitopf*, or meal in a pot, is popular at midday in Berlin. It is a thick pea or lentil soup with sausage.

◀ **The importance of agriculture varies from one country to another within the European Community.**

▲ **The Metzgerei or butcher's shop sells a wide range of different types of sausage.**

# TRADE AND INDUSTRY

▲ *Germany's wealth is based on industrial growth. This development at Godorf on the river Rhine is typical of many throughout the country.*

Germany is one of the world's most successful industrial nations. Huge chemical refineries, iron and steel works, engineering and textile factories, banks and insurance companies have helped to make it a rich, powerful country.

In the 19th century traditional industries such as iron, steel and engineering grew up on coalfields like the Ruhr. At this time Germany's production of steel, ships, railway lines, trains and machines was third only to that of the UK and the USA. These traditional heavy industries developed close to the mines which provided raw materials like iron ore and fuel in the form of coal. Since 1945 most of the traditional industries have been completely rebuilt with modern factories and machines. Over two million people still work in Germany's heavy industries producing cars, trucks, ships,

STEEL PRODUCTION 1990 (million tonnes)

| | |
|---|---|
| 46 | Germany |
| 12 | Belgium |
| 2 | Denmark |
| 3 | Greece |
| 13 | Spain |
| 17 | France |
| 1 | Ireland |
| 23 | Italy |
| 4 | Luxembourg |
| 5 | Netherlands |
| 2 | Portugal |
| 18 | UK |

▲ *Germany is by far the most important European steel producer.*

► *Engineering industries have grown around steel works in areas like the Ruhr, the most important heavy industrial area in Europe.*

robots and a wide range of machines. Many of these goods are exported all over the world for German engineering has an extremely good reputation.

The chemicals industry grew up on the lignite (brown coal) fields. But when oil became the basis of the industry refineries were built along the rivers Rhine and Elbe where the oil could be imported by barge or pipeline. Now the chemicals industry produces a huge range of goods from pharmaceuticals to paints, plastics, insecticides and video tape.

Many new industries have developed since 1945, making goods such as musical instruments and video recorders. These factories are not closely linked to either coalfields or rivers but are described as

FOOTLOOSE because they can be set up almost anywhere. As a result a lot of the new factories have been built in south Germany where there was cheaper land, more space for expansion and a pleasant, unpolluted ENVIRONMENT. Towns such as Stuttgart, Freiburg and Munich have all shared this growth.

Expensive glassware and high quality ceramics are made in both east and south Germany, while almost all towns have workshops making a variety of goods from toys to clothes.

◀ *Modern car factories need lots of space, so they are usually built at the edge of a town where land is cheaper and there is the added advantage of nearby main roads and motorways.*

As the German economy has grown so the country's industrialists have turned to producing new and better products. Consumer goods, such as television sets, washing machines, refrigerators and microwave ovens are manufactured close to large cities like Düsseldorf, Stuttgart, Berlin and Frankfurt. The output of other consumer goods, such as cigarettes, has increased since unification. East Germans were heavy smokers, but health workers hope to reduce the consumption of cigarettes.

Germany also has a reputation for making high quality, precision goods like binoculars, cameras and microscopes. Firms such as Zeiss at Jena are world famous for their optical instruments.

Volkswagen and Mercedes-Benz dominate the German automobile industry. The companies make lorries, vans, buses and trucks as well as cars. The car industry has component factories which each make a particular part, such as gearboxes, engines, spark plugs or axles. These are then taken to the assembly plant and put together on the computer controlled assembly line where robots are

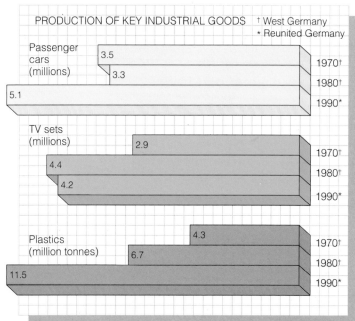

PRODUCTION OF KEY INDUSTRIAL GOODS   † West Germany
                                     * Reunited Germany

| | | |
|---|---|---|
| Passenger cars (millions) | 3.5 | 1970† |
| | 3.3 | 1980† |
| 5.1 | | 1990* |
| TV sets (millions) | 2.9 | 1970† |
| 4.4 | | 1980† |
| | 4.2 | 1990* |
| Plastics (million tonnes) | 4.3 | 1970† |
| 6.7 | | 1980† |
| 11.5 | | 1990* |

# KEY FACTS

● In 1990 Germany produced 5.1 million cars.
● Volkswagen, Europe's fourth largest car producer, is based at Wolfsburg near Brunswick.
● Firms in the west of the country are opening branches in the east where wage rates are lower.

used for many of the tasks. Using robots reduces costs and increases efficiency, but can mean fewer jobs and even unemployment for humans.

After the country was unified in 1990 East German car factories were found to be old and to have inefficient, out-of-date machinery. These factories are now being modernised but the new equipment is expensive and so the modernization is slow. As a result many of the former car workers will be out of work for a considerable time.

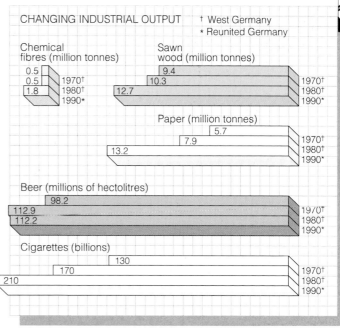

CHANGING INDUSTRIAL OUTPUT  † West Germany  * Reunited Germany

Chemical fibres (million tonnes)
- 0.5 — 1970†
- 0.5 — 1980†
- 1.8 — 1990*

Sawn wood (million tonnes)
- 9.4 — 1970†
- 10.3 — 1980†
- 12.7 — 1990*

Paper (million tonnes)
- 5.7 — 1970†
- 7.9 — 1980†
- 13.2 — 1990*

Beer (millions of hectolitres)
- 98.2 — 1970†
- 112.9 — 1980†
- 112.2 — 1990*

Cigarettes (billions)
- 130 — 1970†
- 170 — 1980†
- 210 — 1990*

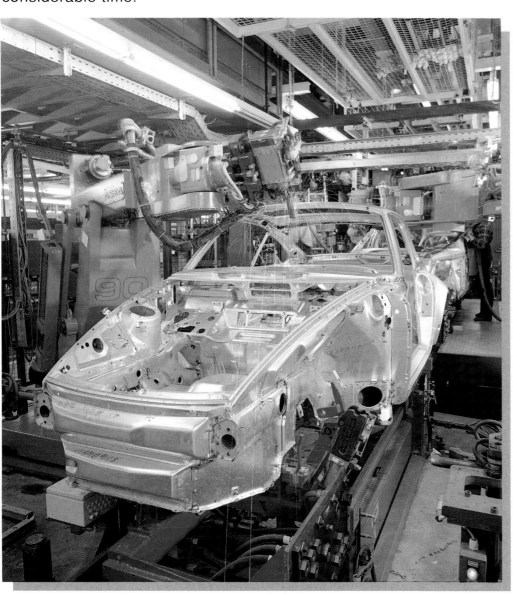

◀ **Germany has a reputation for producing high quality goods, like this Porsche car. High quality engineering is associated with modern design, styling and reliability. One of the reasons for Germany's continued success as an exporter of cars and other manufactured goods is its concentration on high quality, high value products.**

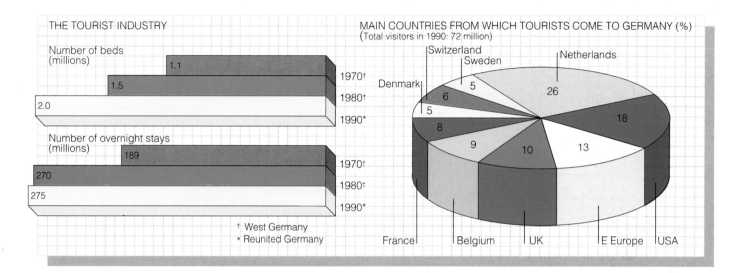

THE TOURIST INDUSTRY

Number of beds
(millions)

| | |
|---|---|
| 1.1 | 1970† |
| 1.5 | 1980† |
| 2.0 | 1990* |

Number of overnight stays
(millions)

| | |
|---|---|
| 189 | 1970† |
| 270 | 1980† |
| 275 | 1990* |

† West Germany
* Reunited Germany

MAIN COUNTRIES FROM WHICH TOURISTS COME TO GERMANY (%)
(Total visitors in 1990: 72 million)

Switzerland 5
Sweden 5
Denmark 6
Netherlands 26
18
5
8
9 10 13
France
Belgium
UK
E Europe
USA

The tourist industry in Germany is based on three main types of resource:

*Natural resources* like the Alps, the rivers, the beaches and the sunshine.

*Cultural resources* which are based on the culture of the local people, especially their way of life, including food, festivals, clothes, castles and dances. Here the traditional regional costumes are important, such as the *lederhosen* (leather trousers), and festivals like *Oktoberfest*.

*Specially-built resources* which include restaurants, hotels, swimming pools, airports and chair-lifts. These have been built to make sure visitors have a good time.

◀ **High quality porcelain has been made in Dresden since the early 18th century. Porcelain is made by baking clay at very high temperatures. Meissen and Dresden are two of the main centres, famous for their beautiful figures, vases, ornaments and tableware. Many of the finest pieces are hand-painted by skilled artists.**

## KEY FACTS

● The average length of stay at German tourist resorts is 5 days.

● In 1990 72 million foreign visitors arrived in Germany.

● Some tourist centres, like Berlin or the Zugspitze mountain, attract large numbers of visitors and are called 'honeypot' sites.

● Germany offers many city-based holidays, beach holidays (eg the Baltic coast), forest holidays (Black Forest), mountain holidays (the Alps), and river holidays (the Rhine and the Elbe).

● Over 18% of Germany's workforce is employed in financial services.

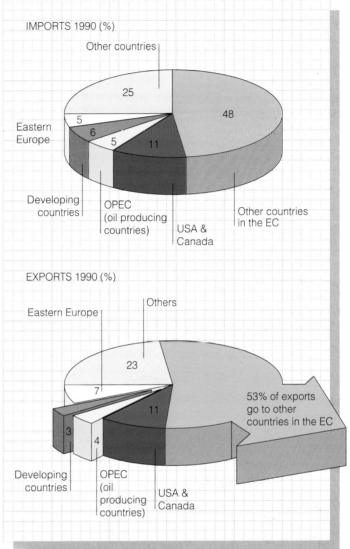

IMPORTS 1990 (%)

Other countries — 25
Eastern Europe — 5
6
5
11
48
Developing countries
OPEC (oil producing countries)
USA & Canada
Other countries in the EC

EXPORTS 1990 (%)

Eastern Europe
Others
23
7
11
3
4
53% of exports go to other countries in the EC
Developing countries
OPEC (oil producing countries)
USA & Canada

Millions of people depend on tourism for their living. Some work in hotels, others in airports, restaurants, as guides or taxi drivers. Farmers close to tourist centres take in visitors and sell some of their food to the tourist hotels. Other people earn a living by making goods like cameras, food, toys or binoculars to sell to the tourists.

Tourism, however, can bring problems as well as wealth. As the number of visitors increases traffic jams become worse in cities like Cologne and Munich. As a result air pollution can become a serious problem.

There is also the danger that traditional forms of dress, music or dance become no more than shows for tourists.

▶ *Every day thousands of stocks and shares are bought and sold on the Frankfurt Stock Exchange. When an economy is growing stocks and shares increase in value, but their value falls when an economy shrinks.*

▲ *Electric trams help to reduce air pollution in cities like Düsseldorf. Tram systems are expensive to build but are popular with commuters and shoppers.*

## KEY FACTS

● In 1990 Germany had 44,080 kilometres of railway line, 10% less than in 1970.

● 33% of families in Germany have two cars and 5% of families have 3 or more cars.

● Each year Germans spend on average DM1,600 on car repairs.

In the 1930s Germany became the first European country to build *autobahnen* (motorways). Although much of the network was damaged in 1945 at the end of the Second World War the routes have been rebuilt and extended. The *autobahnen* in what was East Germany are being improved to match those in the rest of the country.

The Deutsche Bundesbahn (German railways) provide a fast, frequent service between the main towns and cities. This is particularly important because Germany is such a big country. The new high-speed rail line from Berlin to Hanover will cut travelling time by over 30 per cent. New locomotives are faster, heavier and more powerful, enabling 30 per cent of the country's goods traffic to be carried on the railways.

Underground railways in Berlin, Hamburg and Munich are important in getting commuters to and from work. Berlin has two underground systems. The S'Bahn is the older of the two and is being modernised and old stations reopened.

Air travel is popular within Germany because of the country's size. Lufthansa, the national airline, has routes to all main cities from its base in Frankfurt. International routes are based at Berlin and Frankfurt.

Pipelines have recently become an important form of transport, especially for liquids like crude oil.

▶ *The network of canals and navigable rivers like the Rhine carry 25 per cent of Germany's goods. 'Push' barges like this one can move far heavier loads than traditional 'pull' barges.*

### INLAND WATERWAYS (1991)

| | Length of waterways in use (km) | No. of goods vessels | Tonnes carried (millions) |
|---|---|---|---|
| Germany | 4,350 | 2,723 | 231.5 |
| Belgium | 1,951 | 1,778 | 99.4 |
| France | 8,500 | 3,079 | 66.1 |
| Luxembourg | 37 | 25 | 1.1 |
| Netherlands | 5,046 | 9,555 | 286.1 |

▲ **Waterways are important for moving goods around Europe but air transport is vital for the movement of people.**

### CIVIL AVIATION (1990)

| | Number of airlines | Number of aircraft | Passenger kilometres (millions) |
|---|---|---|---|
| Germany | 2 | 162 | 54,645 |
| Belgium | 1 | 30 | 6,761 |
| Denmark | 2 | N/A | 4,223 |
| Greece | 1 | 59 | 8,015 |
| Spain | 1 | 86 | 21,035 |
| France | 4 | 208 | 50,485 |
| Ireland | 2 | N/A | 4,298 |
| Italy | 2 | 88 | 18,298 |
| Luxembourg | 1 | N/A | 138 |
| Netherlands | 3 | N/A | 25,246 |
| Portugal | 1 | 26 | 6,231 |
| UK | 3 | 248 | 63,189 |

# THE ENVIRONMENT

Germans are very aware of the importance of protecting their environment. One of the main environmental threats is from ACID RAIN. Since the 1970s the rain falling on Germany has become more and more acid. All rain contains some acid because the water dissolves gases in the air like sulphur dioxide. Recently, however, the amount of sulphur dioxide in the air has increased. In turn this has made the rain more acid. Acid rain kills fish and plants in rivers and lakes. Trees are damaged or even killed by acid rain, and now half of all the Black Forest trees are affected. Acid rain can be prevented by fitting special filters to power stations. The filters remove the sulphur dioxide, but they are very expensive.

Germany's rivers and lakes are polluted by farms, factories and towns. Chemicals used to control insects or weeds on farms find their way into the water system. When this happens plants, fish and wildlife die. Despite stricter laws factories still sometimes pollute

▲ *Many farmers spray chemicals such as pesticides and artificial fertilisers from the air. Only about 20 per cent of the spray lands on the crops, the rest may be blown away and affect the lungs of people living nearby.*

▶ *Polluted water from a phosphate factory is discharged into the river. Industrial waste can be very toxic, especially that containing heavy metals like cadmium and lead, as well as liquids such as cyanide.*

water supplies. Some sewage and domestic waste from towns along the river Elbe also gets into the rivers.

One of the most recent threats to the environment is the growing use by industry of strong cleaning fluids. These fluids are called polychlorinated biphenyls or PCBs for short and have become important in factories. However when they escape into

# KEY FACTS

● In 1990 Germany produced 297,000 tonnes of pesticides and herbicides.

● In the forests of the Harz mountains some rare animals like the lynx and the wildcat still manage to survive.

● The golden eagle has begun to breed again in the alpine areas of southern Germany.

● Some power stations have special boilers to burn domestic rubbish to generate electricity for local blocks of flats.

● Some buildings are losing 4% of their weight each year as acid rain rots away the brick and stone.

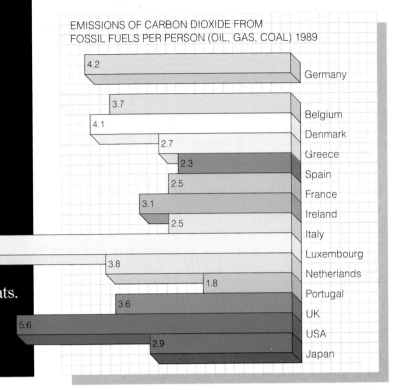

EMISSIONS OF CARBON DIOXIDE FROM FOSSIL FUELS PER PERSON (OIL, GAS, COAL) 1989

|  |  |
|---|---|
| Germany | 4.2 |
| Belgium | 3.7 |
| Denmark | 4.1 |
| Greece | 2.7 |
| Spain | 2.3 |
| France | 2.5 |
| Ireland | 3.1 |
| Italy | 2.5 |
| Luxembourg | 7.4 |
| Netherlands | 3.8 |
| Portugal | 1.8 |
| UK | 3.6 |
| USA | 5.6 |
| Japan | 2.9 |

rivers and lakes they kill all forms of life.
Germany is now trying to control this type
of pollution by imposing heavy fines on
firms which fail to treat their waste properly.

Despite these problems Germany is
improving the environment in many areas.
In the forests of the east and south wild
boar, adders and deer continue to multiply.
The numbers of chamois, a type of deer,

and ibex, a type of goat, are also increasing
in the Alps. Species like the eagle owl, Elbe
beaver, horseshoe bat and wildcat which
were all threatened with extinction now
enjoy special protection.

Even within cities the environment is
being improved by schemes to redevelop
slum areas, or to reduce the volume of
traffic and increase the area of parks and
green space. Cars, lorries and buses are
burning more lead-free petrol, and special
converters fitted to vehicle exhausts are
helping to improve air quality. The nuclear
power programme has been halted because
of the fear of an escape of radioactivity.
Instead, alternative forms of energy which
use wind, water or sunlight are being
developed.

# THE FUTURE

Germany only became a united country in 1871. In 1945 it was again divided and reunification did not come until 1990. Despite all these dramatic changes Germany has become a rich and powerful country whose people enjoy a high standard of living. Because of its size, position and economic strength Germany has become one of the most important

▼ *Advances in modern medicine mean that many more diseases can be treated or cured, and that many more people will live into old age. New techniques, new treatments and new drugs are being developed as a result of research funded by government and industry.*

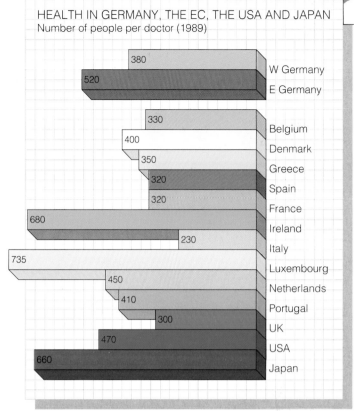

HEALTH IN GERMANY, THE EC, THE USA AND JAPAN
Number of people per doctor (1989)

| Country | Number |
| --- | --- |
| W Germany | 380 |
| E Germany | 520 |
| Belgium | 330 |
| Denmark | 400 |
| Greece | 350 |
| Spain | 320 |
| France | 320 |
| Ireland | 680 |
| Italy | 230 |
| Luxembourg | 735 |
| Netherlands | 450 |
| Portugal | 410 |
| UK | 300 |
| USA | 470 |
| Japan | 660 |

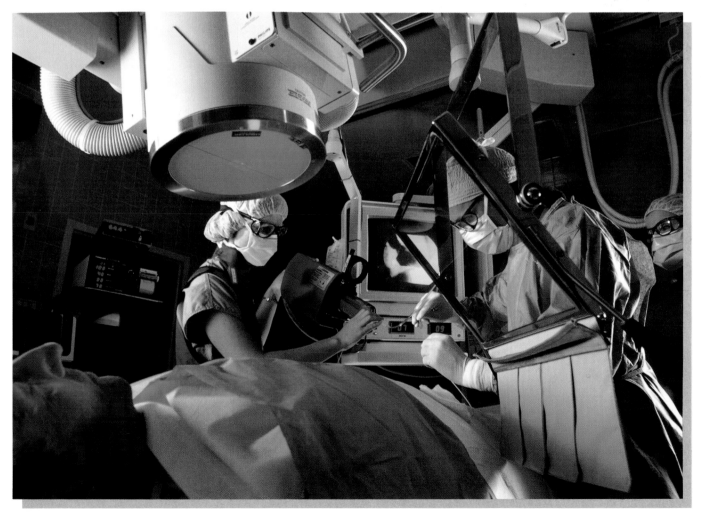

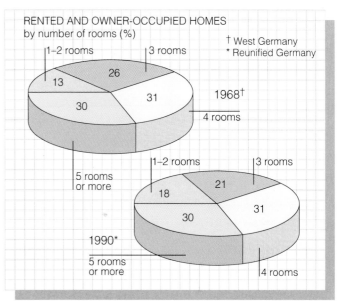

*◀A new building development in what used to be East Berlin*

*▼Since reunification the number of one to two-roomed homes has risen because more East Germans still live in small flats.*

RENTED AND OWNER-OCCUPIED HOMES
by number of rooms (%)

† West Germany
* Reunified Germany

1–2 rooms — 13
3 rooms — 26
4 rooms — 31
5 rooms or more — 30

1968†

1–2 rooms — 18
3 rooms — 21
4 rooms — 31
5 rooms or more — 30

1990*

members of the European Community. This importance is likely to increase as the Community expands its membership.

Within Germany much effort has focused on reducing the difference in standards of living between the eastern and western areas. Farms are being modernised, roads rebuilt and factories re-equipped in the drive to improve conditions in the east.

Planners are struggling to equalise economic opportunities and incomes in the different regions. Aid is poured into the poorer rural areas in the highlands, and parts of the north and east. Nearly half of Germany gets some form of state help.

Between 1945 and 1990 the two parts of Germany were pulled apart. One part was encouraged to look to the West for help, the other to look to the Communist countries in the east. Germany's own identity is only now beginning to emerge since the

reunification of the country. The nation's prosperity, its economic strength and its sense of history will be important factors in the future of both Germany and Europe.

# KEY FACTS

● Germany is spending over DM300 million to reduce problems of noise near motorways and airports.
● Over DM2 billion are being spent building new roads and railways in the eastern parts of Germany.
● Funds from the USA, Canada, Switzerland and the UK are helping to rebuild the eastern parts of Germany.

▶**Although Berlin is many kilometres from the sea, a popular beach has been created around the Wannsee Lake. Here Berliners can relax and improve their suntans, yet still be close to their homes and work. In future people will have more leisure time so other cities will need to build artificial beaches.**

# FURTHER INFORMATION

THE GERMAN NATIONAL TOURIST OFFICE, 65 Curzon Street, London W1Y 7PE. National tourist offices are usually a good source of leaflets and posters.
GERMAN TRAVEL CENTRE, 8 Earlham Street, London WC2H 9RY
GERMAN CHAMBER OF COMMERCE AND INDUSTRY, 16 Buckingham Gate, London SW1E 6LB
THE GOETHE INSTITUTE, London German Cultural Institute, 50 Princes Gate, London SW7 2PG. The best source of information on any aspect of German culture.

Each of the 16 Länder governments has an information office which provides information about the region. The addresses of these offices can be obtained from The Information Department, The German Embassy, 23 Belgrave Square, London SW1X 8PO.

## BOOKS ABOUT GERMANY

Germany was only reunited in 1990, so there are not yet many books on the country since then. The books in this list provide useful background material, although they were written before 1900 and are almost all about West Germany. There was very little accurate information available about East Germany in the West.

*Focus on West Germany*, Albert Macdonald, Hamish Hamilton 1985
*People and Places: Germany*, Macmillan 1987
*Passport to West Germany*, Franklin Watts 1988
*Countries of the World: West Germany*, Wayland 1989
*In Germany*, D Prowse (ed.), Chancerel 1983
*Geographical Studies in Western Europe* (2nd edition), T W Randle, Longman 1987
*Europe Today*, D J Davis and D C Flint, Unwin Hyman 1987

# GLOSSARY

**ACID RAIN**
Rain polluted by gases like sulphur dioxide. Acid rain can cause harm to plants, fish and animals as well as damaging buildings.

**ARABLE FARMING**
Agriculture in which crop-growing is the farmer's main source of income.

**ABITUR**
Examination taken by pupils at 18 to win a university place.

**BUNDESRAT**
The upper house of the German Parliament.

**BUNDESTAG**
The lower house of the German Parliament.

**CIS**
The Commonwealth of Independent States. It consists of many of the states that were once part of the USSR.

**COLLECTIVE FARMS**
Farms in East Germany which were owned by the state.

**DAIRY FARMING**
Agriculture which concentrates on rearing cattle to produce milk, cream, butter and cheese.

**ENVIRONMENT**
All the things that surround people, such as buildings and natural landscape.

**FARMING CO-OPERATIVES**
System in which farmers join together to share costs.

**FOOTLOOSE INDUSTRY**
Industries which are not tied to using one source of power or raw material such as coal or iron ore and so can be started in a wide variety of places.

**FOREIGN WORKERS**
People who have moved from one country to another in order to find work (previously referred to as guest workers).

**GYMNASIUM**
One of the three types of German secondary school. The word means 'grammar school', it does not refer to the school's sports facilities.

**HAUPTSCHULE**
One of the three types of secondary school.

**LÄNDER**
The 16 states which make up Germany.

**LANGLAUF**
Cross-country skiing; shorter skies enable skiers to trek up and down hills.

**LIGNITE**
Brown coal; it is softer than black coal but will burn to generate heat.

**OPEC**
The Organization of Petroleum Exporting Countries. It consists of most of the world's main oil-producing countries.

**OPEN-CAST MINING**
Mining from open pits (particularly lignite).

**PESTICIDES**
Chemicals used to kill pests that might harm crops.

**REALSCHULE**
One of the three types of secondary school.

**RENEWABLE ENERGY**
Energy based on power sources which will not run out, such as the wind, waves and the sun.

**WEINFEST**
Celebration at the end of the grape harvest.

# INDEX

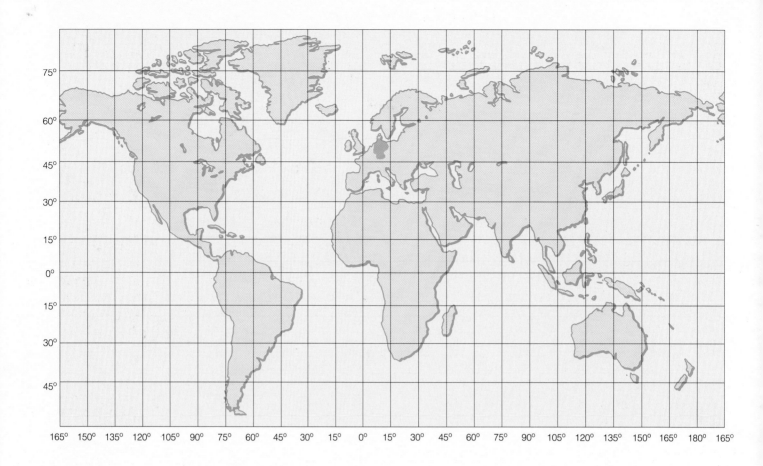